Giving Grace

One Pastor's Journey through False Accusations

John Amankwatia

Kingdom Publishers

Copyright© John Amankwatia 2024

All rights reserved. No part of this book may be reproduced in any form by photocopying or any electronic or mechanical means, including information storage or retrieval systems, without permission in writing from both the copyright owner and the publisher of the book. The right of John Amankwatia to be identified as the author of this work has been asserted by him in accordance with the Copyright, Designs and Patents Act 1988 and any subsequent amendments thereto.

A catalogue record for this book is available from the British Library.

All scripture quotations have been taken from the New Century version of the Bible

ISBN: 978-1-916801-15-8

1st Edition 2024 by Kingdom Publishers, London, UK.

You can purchase copies of this book from any leading bookstore or email contact@kingdompublishers.co.uk

Dedicated to Edward and Rachel - God's gifts to me.

Children are a gift from the Lord;
babies are a reward.

Psalm 127:3 (NCV)

Contents

Preface	9
Introduction	11
Chapter One	
Unveiling the Schemes of Satan	15
Recognising the Enemy's Tactics	16
Chapter Two	
The Shepherd and the Widow	20
Offering Solace and Support	20
Chapter Three	
Generosity Repaid with Grief	27
The Request for Return	28
Chapter Four	
A Spiritually Orchestrate Trap	33
The Accusation Emerges	33
The Agony of Misunderstood Intentions	34
Chapter Five	
The Trial of False Witness	37
Confronting the Allegations	37
The Emotional Toll of Injustice	38
Chapter Six	
Clinging to Faith Amidst the Storm	42
Standing Firm in Beliefs	42
The Role of Prayer and Community	43
Chapter Seven	
Navigating the Legal Labyrinth	47
The Pastor's Defence	47
Legal Obstacles and Triumphs	49

Chapter Eight

The Church's Reaction to Scandal — 53
   Maintaining Unity — 53
   Handling Dissension Within the Flock — 54

Chapter Nine

The Lessons of Job Revisited — 57
   Patience and Endurance in Suffering — 58
   Finding Peace in Divine Wisdom — 59

Chapter Ten

The Long Road to Vindication — 63
   Awaiting Justice — 63
   The Power of Forgiveness in Healing — 64

Chapter Eleven

Educating the Flock on Satan's Realities — 67
   Preventing Future Missteps — 67
   Equipping the Church with Knowledge — 68

Chapter Twelve

Continuing the Pastoral Call — 72
   Moving Beyond the Ordeal — 72
   Refocusing on Ministry and Outreach — 73
   Emerging Stronger in Faith and Purpose — 76

Appendix A

Resources for the Accused — 79

Appendix B

Scriptures for Comfort and Defence — 81

Appendix C

Recognising the Spiritual Warfare Around Us — 84
About the Author — 86

Preface

Reverend David Thompson (Pastor Thom) had always been a man of faith, dedicated to serving his congregation and spreading the word of God. But his faith was about to be tested in ways he never imagined. It all started with a monetary gift from an appreciative recipient of his pastoral support or so he thought. Mrs Johnson had lost her husband, and Pastor Thom had offered her guidance and support during those difficult times. Feeling grateful for the support, she gave him a monetary gift.

A year later, Mrs Johnson approached Pastor Thom to return her money. Although surprised by the request, Pastor Thom (Thom) obliged and returned the monetary gift. However, to Thom's shock and dismay, Mrs. Johnson made an unexpected move a few years later. She reported to the church authorities that Pastor Thom had been defrauding congregation members. She claimed that he had coerced her into giving him the monetary gift and that Pastor Thom had been taking advantage of other vulnerable members as well. Of course, Pastor Thom was distraught as the accusations were completely unfounded and contrary to his character and principles.

Mrs Johnson also fabricated another story of a sexual assault, claiming that the Pastor had taken advantage of her vulnerability. Mrs. Johnson brought in the police to investigate, and Pastor Thom fully cooperated by supplying evidence and testimonies to refute the false allegations. After a thorough investigation, the police dismissed the allegations due to lack of evidence, and Pastor Thom was cleared of any wrongdoing.

Despite the police dismissing the claims, the church convened a disciplinary panel to address the situation. After careful consideration and testimonies from both parties, the panel dismissed the sexual assault allegations, finding no evidence to support Mrs. Johnson's claims. However, they held that the Pastor should not have accepted the monetary gift, citing it as a potential conflict of interest. Thom felt betrayed by the church to which he had dedicated his life. They had no policies or codes of conduct in place, yet he was still held responsible for accepting a gift from who he had thought to be a grateful individual.

Amid the chaos, Pastor Thom turned to prayer, knowing that only God could help him in this situation. Thom prayed and received a message of grace and strength. He realised that he needed to trust in God and not his own abilities. He knew that God had used this trial to teach him the importance of prayer, fellowship and divine wisdom in maintaining his integrity and purpose. Through his journey, Thom learned that Satan, the enemy, operates in subtle ways to deceive and destroy. He was reminded of the power of prayer and the importance of having a solid support system.

Most importantly, he experienced firsthand the grace of God, who is always there to guide and protect those who trust Him.

Giving Grace is a story of one man's struggles and a powerful reminder for all pastors and Christians to watch out for the enemy's wiles. It is a call to remain steadfast in faith, seek wisdom from above, and never lose sight of God's grace, even during the darkest times.

Introduction

In the walk of faith, we find ourselves in an arena where unseen forces are at play; where good and evil engage in a perennial tussle for our souls. There is a foe we know all too well among the fold of Christendom, albeit often underestimating his cunning and craft: Satan, the adversary.

For the Christian, awareness of his machinations isn't just advisable; it is imperative. As Christians striding along the path of righteousness, we tend to focus on the luminous prospect of grace and fellowship. Yet, amidst this focus, we can't afford to be naive about the darker shades that lurk just around the corner. Strategies exist devised to ensnare those who would do good, spinning webs of deception in which the kindest of acts can, quite ironically, become a precipice for a fall. It is essential, then, that we illuminate the shadowy corners where Satan operates.

This book delves into the grim reality that the evil one is not just a fable consigned to the archives of ancient texts but a force actively plotting demise in the contemporary. The goal here isn't to incite fear but to foster a sharpness of Spirit, an acuity that empowers pastors and believers alike to identify and outmanoeuvre these sinister plots. Historically, the church has been a beacon of generosity and compassion, a sanctuary where the weary find rest and the burdened receive solace. This book explores how even the noblest intentions can be tainted and twisted by malevolent intents. We must grapple with the notion that our acts of kindness do not exist in a void but on a spiritual battlefield where they can be *weaponised* against us.

Throughout this book, we will traverse a landscape pockmarked with pitfalls created by the accuser. However, let us not misconstrue this journey as a fear-mongering venture. Instead, see it as an odyssey towards enlightenment, one that acquaints us with the true nature of our adversary so that we might stand firm against him.

Let us unwrap the subtle and often overlooked ways that temptations and accusations can present themselves, intercepting them before they bloom into full-fledged spiritual crises. We'll learn how to discern when a situation is not merely unpleasant, but a meticulously crafted snare set by the Enemy.

We are called to be as wise as serpents and as innocent as doves, navigating life's challenges with a calm alertness that befits the inheritors of the Kingdom. This balanced perspective will equip us to extend our hands in generosity without loosening the shield of faith that guards our hearts. Understanding the complexity of this spiritual warfare requires a grounded and practical theology. We'll examine how good intentions can be misinterpreted through real-life scenarios, leading to trials that test our resolve and faith.

We'll witness how a seemingly straightforward act of charity can evolve into an ordeal that places one under the harsh spotlight of judgment and accusation. Steadfastness amidst such tribulations is not innate but one honed through spiritual discipline and community support. The book will underscore the significance of prayer, fellowship, and divine wisdom in upholding one's integrity and purpose during such testing times.

The journey through these pages will also navigate the intricate corridors of legal and public opinion, the nuances of keeping ecclesial unity amidst scandals, and the learning that can guide us forward more robust and equipped than before. We'll draw parallels with the tribulations of Job, conducive to understanding the sanctifying power of endurance. No suffering is wasted in the grand tapestry of God's plan, and every tear holds the potential for growth and deeper communion with the Divine.

Ultimately, the narrative arcs towards forgiveness and healing, showcasing that vindication is not solely a matter of clearing one's name but also a process of inner transformation and reconciliation. It'll cast light on the resilience of an unfaltering grip on God's promises and the importance of nurturing a spirit that forgives as freely as it has been forgiven.

Our discourse will culminate in equipping the church with the necessary insight to recognise and repel the stratagems of Satan, fostering an environment where future missteps are pre-empted and where the Body of Christ stands vigilant and unassailable. We appear not merely as survivors of spiritual warfare but as warriors refined by fire, carrying an awareness that secures us against the Enemy's deceit. We continue our pastoral call, not in the shadow of past ordeals but illuminated by the light of experience, pressing onwards to minister and outreach with renewed purpose.

So, we embark on this expository voyage, not in trepidation but in resolution, knowing that to be forewarned is to be forearmed. Let us take this step together, alert and undaunted, treading confidently in the assurance that He who is in us is more significant than he who is in the world.

Chapter One

Unveiling the Schemes of Satan

Having laid the foundation with our introduction, we now venture into the crucial task of shedding light on the deceptive tactics of the adversary. It is essential to grasp that our enemy isn't playing a game of mere mischief, but waging war tailored to trip us up, often using our most noble intentions as bait in his snare.

Apostle Peter writes *the devil is working against you. He is walking around like a hungry lion with his mouth open. He is looking for someone [you] to eat* (1 Peter 5:8, NLV, brackets mine). The schemes of Satan are a dizzying web woven into our everyday experiences with such subtlety that we can easily be blindsided by their influence. My task isn't to invoke fear but to awaken discernment, for it is through understanding the delicate threads of temptation and accusation that Satan weaves that we can learn not to be ensnared by them.

So, let us pull back the veil and begin our journey to outwit the sly master of lies of whom John writes *the devil has nothing to do with the truth. There is no truth in him. It is expected of the devil to lie, for he is a liar and the father of lies'*(John 8:44), by first recognising the ways he lingers near, ready to twist our kindness into weapons of our own downfall.

Recognising the Enemy's Tactics

We must be clued up on the enemy's manoeuvres in spiritual warfare. As you've journeyed with me thus far, grasping that Satan isn't slack in craftiness is pivotal. He'll slip in — sly as a fox — twisting truth and sowing seeds of dismay. His ability lies in deception, hiding behind seemingly innocent encounters, all the while setting the stage for your downfall. His tactics aren't just brash or blatant; they're often cloaked under layers of normalcy.

When we open our hearts in generosity, we must be alert, lest our kindness become the foothold the adversary yearns for. Remember, it is not the grand gestures where we're most vulnerable, but in the day-to-day interactions where we let our guard down. Vigilance, therefore, becomes our watchword as we stand firm, equipped with discernment that outwits the snares laid subtly in our path. The Message Bible puts the Apostle Peter's warning beautifully, Keep *a cool head. Stay alert.* (1 Peter 5:8a)

The Subtlety of Temptation and Accusation dives deep into understanding how the adversary cleverly intertwines temptation and accusation to ensnare God's children. It is an intricate dance, where often the music is so low that we can barely hear the steps, we're meant to take, and therein lies the trap.

Consider the nature of temptation — it is hardly ever a blatant call to do evil. It is quiet, a whispered suggestion, softly nudging us towards a seemingly harmless decision. It is that extra minute glance at what we ought not to, the rationalising of a minor indiscretion, or that justification for bending the truth. The subtlety lies in the deception that these actions are of little consequence. But here lies the groundwork for the next phase — accusation.

Once we succumb to temptation, Satan assumes a new role, that of the accuser. Before God, he charges us with the sins he lured us into committing (Revelation 12:10). It is a sly tactic that leaves many feelings defenceless and defeated. They have been led to a pit and then blamed for falling in...

The effectiveness of Satan's strategy is rooted in its covert nature. He tiptoes around our conscience, weakening our resolve until the line between right and wrong is blurred. After yielding to temptation, individuals may find that their reputation is tarnished. Accusation amplifies the indiscretion, often stirred in public opinion or within the internal dialogue of the conscience, leaving the believer disoriented. Those who walk in faith are not oblivious to Satan's schemes. However, awareness alone does not make one immune to his tactics.

The Bible warns us that the devil prowls like a roaring lion, looking for someone to devour. In the subtleties of his approach, he often finds his prey unguarded. Faithful stewards must, therefore, remain vigilant. It is no coincidence that we find ourselves inexplicably under scrutiny just when we've offered a helping hand or extended grace. Satan's timing is precise, striking when we're teetering on the cusp of impacting the Kingdom positively.

The role of the community in detecting such deceptions must be considered. A body of believers connected and in tune with the Holy Spirit, can serve as an early warning system for those undergoing temptation. Furthermore, once the cycle has advanced to accusation, it falls upon the church to rise in support of its members and not be quick to cast the first stone. Scripture has equipped us for these moments.

What is often overlooked is the subtlety of these wiles. At first glance, they often appear as reasonable, harmless, or even righteous acts. But beneath the surface, they may contradict God's word. The paths of temptation and accusation are filled with nuance; they often intertwine with everyday life's complexities. One moment we stand offering the hand of fellowship; the next, we find ourselves accused, our actions misinterpreted through a distorted lens. It is critical to remember that Satan's accusations often distort the truths of our actions.

What was done in love and obedience to God can be twisted to appear self-serving or destructive. The enemy's narrative can be so persuasive that even the most devout can question their intentions.

The whispers of accusation can also spread like wildfire through a congregation, igniting gossip and suspicion. Before we know it, Satan has not just ensnared an individual but has sown discord among the brethren. The unity of the church is threatened by doubt and fear. In such times, grounding one's self in the word and reminding oneself of God's promises is essential.

We're informed that *there is now no condemnation to them which are in Christ Jesus* (Romans 8:1), providing a solid defence against the sense of blame that accusation instils. Moreover, an internal patrol of our hearts can prepare us for these assaults. By regularly examining our motives and aligning our actions with Scripture, we strengthen our defences against the temptations that lead to accusation. It is a preventive measure, allowing the shields of faith to quench the fiery darts before they ignite.

We also must understand that the aim of these diabolical strategies is not merely to discredit us but ultimately to distract us from our mission. When we're busy defending ourselves against accusations, our focus shifts from the work of the Kingdom to the work of clearing our name.

Let us know the subtleties, employing discernment and wisdom as our guides. In doing so, we stand not as easy targets but as warriors equipped for battle, recognising that our struggle is not against flesh and blood but against spiritual forces of evil in the heavenly realms. In this struggle, we must cling to the truth that we are more than conquerors in Christ, and no accusation nor temptation can separate us from His love (Romans 8:38-39).

Chapter Two

The Shepherd and the Widow

Slipping through the cracks of our best intentions, the adversary often masks his snares in the visage of virtue, preying on the compassionate. There's a tale, as old as time, of a shepherd – a pastor – who, led by a heartfelt call to serve, extended his hand to a widow in distress. This widow cloaked in sorrow and seemingly in need of aid, found solace in the support of the church's shepherd. But let us pause for a moment and consider what if the widow's grief is but a facade and her plight a strategic play in a more sinister game.

This chapter delves into the intricate dance of kindness and deceit and reflects on how Satan exploits good deeds, twisting them into bonds that could fetter even the most vigilant believer. So, we can't simply walk away; we have to equip our hearts with wisdom and discernment, offer comfort without compromising our guard, and truly understand the motivation behind every gift – lest we unwittingly step into a trap laid with the threads of our generosity.

Offering Solace and Support

In the wake of this twisted situation, we must remember the heart of Christ for those bruised and battered by life's harsh winds. Our shepherd's instinct should be to offer refuge, like the widow seeking solace, knocking at the door of her pastor's compassion. Yet, in the warmth of such support, there lurks a peril, for even in acts of kindness, the serpent coils, ready to strike.

It is not about encouraging paranoia but a sobering reminder that the enemy can twist our good intentions. We must then navigate with wisdom rooted in prayer, our actions bathed in discernment. Offering a hand should never lead to an open door for the accuser, so we tread this path with caution and unwavering love, offering solace in a world where support can be a double-edged sword.

The Motivation Behind the Gift

Often, we see acts of kindness and generosity as outward expressions of inner goodwill. And justifiably so, it is a reflection of the heart's abundance. But as we walk the narrow path, we must be discerning. Why? Because sometimes the intention stitched into the fabric of a gift is not as clear-cut as we might assume.

Let us consider Pastor Thom and Mrs Johnson's case.

Pastor Thom offered guidance and support for Mrs. Johnson during difficult times, including counselling and comfort, and she held him in high regard. Feeling grateful for her support, Mrs. Johnson gave Pastor Thom a monetary gift to show her appreciation for his kindness and leadership. To avoid any future misunderstanding and to have a receipt, Pastor Thom insisted the money was credited to his bank account. A year later, Mrs Johnson, maybe regretting her decision to give the gift, approached Pastor Thom to return her money. Although surprised by the request, Pastor Thom obliged. However, to Pastor Thom's shock and dismay, Mrs. Johnson made an unexpected move a few years later. She reported to the church authorities that Pastor Thom had been defrauding congregation members.

She claimed that he had coerced her into giving him the monetary gift and that he had been taking advantage of other vulnerable members as well. Of course, the accusations were completely unfounded and contrary to Pastor Thom's character and principles. To his further dismay, Mrs Johnson also fabricated a story of a sexual assault, claiming that the pastor had taken advantage of her vulnerability. Mrs. Johnson brought in the police to investigate, and Pastor Thom fully cooperated, supplying evidence and testimonies to refute the false allegations.

To make matters worse, one of Pastor Thom's colleagues also reported to the investigators that he had defrauded the church without evidence. After a thorough examination, the police dismissed the allegations due to lack of evidence, and Pastor Thom was cleared of any wrongdoing. Despite dismissing the allegations, the church convened a disciplinary panel to address the situation. After careful consideration and testimonies from both parties, the panel dismissed the sexual assault allegations, finding no evidence to support Mrs. Johnson's claims. However, they held that the pastor should not have accepted the monetary gift.

Pastor Thom was deeply hurt by the entire ordeal because the church had no policies or codes of conduct in place, so he accepted Mrs Johnson's gift with gratitude. Of course, Thom knew that his position and role had high expectations of him, which until Mrs Johnson complaint; he had discharged without any incident. Rick Warren correctly points out, 'Criticism is the cost of influence. As long as you don't influence anybody, nobody is going to say a peep about you. But the greater your influence... the more critics you are going to have.'[1]

Pastor Thom accepted and knew that his private and public actions were always under scrutiny, so he realised that sometimes even a

---

[1] Warren, Rick (1995). The Purpose Driven Church. Grand Rapids, MI: Zondervan.

well-intentioned action can have unforeseen consequences. However, we can easily fall into the trap of judging others including pastors on a superficial basis, just as Elihu, Job's friend does. Beware of the dangers of criticising others. Be very careful of what we say about other people. And if you are on the receiving end of criticism, don't be surprised.

Pastor Thom had dedicated his life to serving his congregations with integrity and compassion, and the false accusations had deeply shaken him. However, guided by his faith and principles, he forgave Mrs. Johnson, his colleague, and the church authorities. Despite his challenges, Pastor Thompson continued to preach the gospel of the crucified and the resurrected Christ with unwavering dedication. Christian friends familiar with the case rallied around him, offering their support and understanding. Together, they worked to heal the wounds caused by the ordeal, ultimately emerging more robust and focused than before. Through forgiveness, resilience, and the support of his congregation, Pastor Thom showed the power of faith and compassion in overcoming adversity.

It is saddening but confirmed that an obscured motive can sometimes lurk behind a benevolent smile. Solace and support, the hallmarks of a caring community, can sometimes be mistaken for weakness or ulterior motives. Indeed, the widow's mite was untainted by agenda; however, not every act of giving mirrors such purity. We must ask ourselves if every gift is given to bless, or could there be a more profound, perhaps darker, rationale? We must be vigilant against the Enemy's schemes, questioning the motivation behind a gift we might receive.

Consider when a gift ultimately outweighs the depth of your relationship with the giver. Could it be that behind this unexpected generosity lies the lure of complacency, a false sense of security, or manipulation? Our adversary can turn even the most sacred actions into a tool for downfall. It is an ancient tactic but ever so practical.

To illustrate, recall the story of the snake in Eden. It didn't just bring an apple but a gift, wrapped in deception — a promise of enlightenment and wisdom. Can the gifts we meet camouflage a similar snare? The generosity we show and receive within our faith communities should ideally reflect the selfless love of our Saviour. We give because we are moved by compassion, not seeking return, not with the slightest hint of bribe, nor to bind another in debt or obligation. Yet, we must admit that the whispers of pride and desire for influence can infiltrate the purest intentions.

As recipients of generosity, it is crucial to examine the Spirit in which the gift is given. If someone gives with the expectation of something in return, be cautious. This doesn't necessarily signal evil but certainly opens the door to complications. Recall the words of Proverbs, which warn that *a gift given in secret can soothe anger, and even a present in a cloak can bring great favour* (Proverbs 21:14).

It is not unheard of for gifts to be used as pawns in a wider strategy, to curry favour or to garner a specific outcome. Power dynamics can often play out subtly within our interactions, and gifts can sometimes be more than just acts of charity — they may serve as transactions in disguise. Considering the giver's history and usual or normal patterns of behaviour can also be enlightening. Have they been known to give generously without any underhanded reasons, or does history reveal a trail of manipulative giving? Understanding the pattern of someone's giving can help us discern his or her true motivation.

Discernment is a gift of the Spirit that we should earnestly covet, especially in these instances. Let us also not shy away from seeking advice from trusted believers. Pastor Thom failed in this regard. If only he had discussed the generosity of Mrs Johnson with a colleague or mature Christian, the outcome might have been different. Discussion among the spiritually mature can sometimes shed light on areas to which we may be blind, particularly when it comes to gifts that come out of the blue or from unfamiliar sources.

Now, in a world that cries out for transparency and authenticity, it isn't always comfortable to question someone's motives. And yet, our calling requires us to be as wise as serpents while still being as innocent as doves. This is particularly relevant when the gift in question might put you in someone else's debt or seem to aim at buying your influence or loyalty. Moreover, the timing of a gift can also speak volumes. Is the gift offered at a time when the giver stands to receive help from your goodwill or decision-making power? These questions are uncomfortable, but they are necessary for the discerning believer.

Ultimately, we must leave room for the possibility that a gift is just a gift — given from the overflow of God's love in a person's heart. However, it is prudent to remember that even in our giving and receiving, we must be alert and prayerful, lest we fall into the enemy's trap. In essence, the motivation behind the gift reflects the heart — it uncovers intention, unveils purpose, and sometimes unmasks an agenda. We would do well to remember that every perfect gift is from above and comes without the shadow of turning. Let us seek that purity in both our giving and our receiving. Hence, it stands to reason that the fruits of the Spirit should be our measuring rod. Gifts given in love, joy, peace, forbearance, kindness, goodness, faithfulness, gentleness, and self-control carry the mark of divine authorship. May we cherish such gifts and aim to mirror them in our own acts of generosity.

So, as we continue on our faith journey, let us maintain a posture of gratefulness for every blessing while exercising wisdom and discernment. Only then can we ensure that our hearts, and those of our Christian friends, remain guarded against the subtle yet harmful motivations that may be interwoven in seemingly innocent offerings.

Chapter Three

Generosity Repaid with Grief

It is a tough pill to swallow, isn't it? When you reach out with an open hand and find it slapped away, the sting can reverberate to the very core of your spirit. We find ourselves questioning why acts of altruism sometimes, paradoxically, return to us as deep wounds. There's a stark lesson in these moments, made more apparent amidst the narrative arc of pastoral care. As discussed above, Thom is a well-meaning pastor animated by a spirit of charity who extends support to a struggling soul (Mrs Johnson) on behalf of the church — but lo and behold, the kind gesture gets twisted.

Malicious intent, like a serpent in the grass, can hijack the fruits of our kindness, turning them into a tool for one's downfall. When that generosity is met with grievance rather than gratitude, it is as if the soft soil in which you planted a seed of goodwill becomes a quicksand of sorrows. This is no mere misfortune; it is a scheme thick with the smoke of spiritual warfare. As followers of Christ, we must tread with the wisdom of serpents and the innocence of doves, keenly aware that our benevolence, though ordained by Scripture, can become the battlefield upon which we're laid bare and vulnerable to attack. Let us delve deep into the heart of this bewilderment: a generosity so pure yet painfully repaid with grief.

Understanding Unforeseen Consequences

Our generous acts can hatch unexpected trials in our endeavour to walk in righteousness. It is a sorrowful truth that even in our most altruistic moments, there can lurk seeds of turmoil. When we give from the heart, whether it be time, resources, or empathy, we're not always privy to the ripple effects of those actions. This chapter tackles the harsh reality that our gifts, when intertwined with the adversary's web, might turn against us, leading to a cascade of grief we hadn't fathomed. It is a sobering reminder that while the call to be Christ-like in our generosity stands firm, we must also stay vigilant, discerning, and prepared for the complexities our kindness may unwittingly forge amidst a world where the prince of deceit manipulates good intentions for his own divisive agenda.

The Request for Return
At the heart of many a trial that visits upon the generous soul, is a scenario that might be as old as humanity itself, and yet, its sting is still as sharp as ever. Picture the scene: Pastor Thom's well-intentioned act of kindness is met, not with gratitude, but a confounding request—or demand—for the return of a gift given in appreciation of his pastoral support. Of course, it was never his practice to expect or receive gifts of any kind from his administration of pastoral care. However, an unexpected twist appears within the haven of support and solace.

Mrs Johnson, once the receiver of Pastor Thom's goodwill, turns about with a claim that she wanted her monetary gift back. This is no mere change of heart but smacks of more malevolent influence, a deception breeds in the shadows. Consider the shock and dismay that grips Pastor Thom. One's compassion is suddenly reframed as naïveté. Yet, in this moment of betrayal, it is here that Satan's ploy becomes clear.

It is a script written by an adversary who knows no bounds in manipulating human frailty. The return request is not just a call for the physical retrieval of that which was gifted; it is an assault on trust, an inversion of intent. It pierces the spirit, aiming to embitter the soul against future acts of generosity. For Satan, it is a two-fold victory: he wounds both the giver and chokes off potential blessings for others. In such moments, the darkness whispers deceit, suggesting that all kindness is folly. A corrosive doubt tries to lodge itself within the mind, a foul seed that, if left unchecked, might grow to sap the vigour of faith itself.

To respond with haste or anger would only further his dark aims. Wisdom, then, is found in patience, in seeking the counsel of the Holy Spirit to discern the true nature of this request. Is it a genuine need misunderstood, or is it, as sometimes revealed, a snare meticulously laid out? One must not rush to judgment but rather to prayerful contemplation.

The response must be neither blind acquiescence nor hard-hearted refusal. There's a delicate balance to strike, where one maintains their integrity and the essence of Christ's love yet refuses to be exploited by the devious mechanisms of evil. Let me spell it out clearly: such scenarios can sow discord within the community. When private generosity becomes public contention, it is as though Satan delights in the ripples of disruption spread through previously calm waters. The pious are pitted against one another, their attention diverted from the mission field to the battleground of petty disputes.

It is not to suggest that every request for recompense is borne of wicked intentions. Humanity, in its complexity, hosts a myriad of reasons that lead one to retract one's first gratitude. Distress, pride, or plain misunderstanding can usher one down this path. One must stand firm in wisdom, ready to separate the wheat from the chaff. Those at the eye of such a storm must gird themselves with scriptural truths.

The Apostle Paul writes, *Though we live in the world, we do not wage war as the world does, meaning the weapons we fight with are not those in this world. We have the divine power to demolish strongholds, including arguments and every pretension that sets itself up against the knowledge of God.* (2 Corinthians 10:3-5). Thus, our defence in this warfare is the divine power coupled with the divine assurance that the Lord shall not forsake those of us who walk uprightly with Him (Psalm 84:11)

Like Job, who stood amidst his trials with unwavering faith, we are called to hold true to our convictions. The insidiousness of Satan's schemes is such that he does not always run with grand gestures of malice. Often, it is within the confines of mundane interactions, turning the trivial into the tumultuous. Be sharp; therefore, be vigilant; the deceitful one takes no rest. At this impasse, the community becomes a sanctuary. It is vital to bring such situations into the light, seeking advice and support from those rooted in the faith.

A shared burden is lightened, and clarity often appears in the gathering of fellow believers. Otherwise, the path of the accused is lonesome, yet it must not be walked in solitude.

Pastor Thom's world crashed when Mrs Johnson and his colleague accused him of defrauding his congregation. The church board suspended him, leaving him with a shattered reputation and heart. Unable to worship at the church he had ministered, Thom felt lost and vulnerable. But amidst the chaos, he found solace in his family and unexpected places.

A neighbouring church welcomed him with open arms and offered him a place to worship and pray. He also found comfort in the company of those who had also been falsely accused, some of whom were not Christians. As time passed, some of these kind souls passed away, leaving Thom with a heavy heart. But he found strength in the words of a website for the Wrongly Accused men[2], reminding him to stay strong and hold his head high. He took their advice and started dressing smartly, not to impress anyone, but to show that he was still God's noble vessel (2 Timothy 2:20-21).

Through this challenging journey, Pastor Thom learned that even in the darkest times, there are always pockets of light and hope. With the support of his family, new church family and the encouraging words from the Wrongly Accused website, he rose above the storm and continued serving the Lord with all his heart. As the investigation continued, Thom feared that the church's action or inaction towards his family could harm their faith. The colleagues he considered friends and with whom he had shared his heart vanished into thin air as if associating with him would tarnish their image. He had seen it happen when other ministers or Christians fell from grace, and their families were left to fend for themselves.

What hurt him the most was the hypocrisy of some of his colleagues, who quickly judged and condemned him without knowing the whole story. They acted as if they were above such temptations, forgetting that even the most righteous can fall. Pastor Thom knew that the Bible warned against self-righteousness and reminded believers to be humble and careful not to fall into temptation (1 Corinthians 10:12, Galatians 6:1). He had always preached this message, but now he saw it being tested in his own life. He prayed for strength and guidance, knowing he could trust God's faithfulness regardless of the investigation's outcome. He prayed for his family that they would not lose their faith in God; that they would find comfort in His love and grace.

---

[2] FACT: Supporting Victims of Unfounded Allegations of Abuse. Available at: https://factuk.org/how-to-cope/how-to-cope-after-a-false-allegation/ (Accessed in 2023).

Ultimately, the investigation cleared Pastor Thom of wrongdoing, and he was reinstated. But the experience had changed him, making him more empathetic towards those who have fallen and more aware of the dangers of pride and judgment. He continued to preach the message of forgiveness and grace, knowing that he needed God's grace and forgiveness. The church is where all are welcome, regardless of past mistakes, because that is what Christ teaches us.

As the body of Christ (the Church), believers are bonded in support and love, exemplifying the grace that is all too absent in the world. We are encouraged to bear one another's burdens, fulfilling the law of Christ. Each trial is a chapter, not the entirety of one's story. And so, Pastor Thom's experience challenges us personally and tests the fabric of any Christian community. Will we allow Satan's seeds to sprout division or weed them out with the unity of the spirit? The enemy wishes to see the generous heart closed, the helping hand withdrawn, and watch as distrust spreads its gnarled roots through the fertile soil. Our response must be to cling tighter to our shield of faith; to let neither kindness be snuffed out nor mercy become a casualty in this unseen warfare. In embracing our Lord's sovereignty, let us stand assured that all things hidden shall in time come to light, and truth, as it always does, will maintain its victorious reign.

Chapter Four

A Spiritually Orchestrate Trap

Transitioning from the shock of a good deed turned sour, we delve into an even darker reality. It is a harsh awakening to acknowledge that our genuine acts of kindness can become snares set by the enemy. How easily a caring hand extended can be twisted, turning a benefactor into a target for scorn. Picture this: a trap, not of metal and springs, but of spirits and intentions, expertly laid out to catch the unwary. It is like walking into a spider's web, glistening with morning dew, only to find you are bound and helpless.

The stage is set, and the unwary soul steps in, thinking they're answering a call of distress, not realising they've become the focus of a spiritual debacle. The accuser doesn't play fair and never sleeps, prowling around, *weaponising* our virtues against us. In a moment, we're caught in the throes of a conflict which is not against flesh and blood but against powers and principalities. Awareness is pivotal; the enemy's tactics are sly, and his webs are spun with deceit that can catch even the most vigilant among us.

The Accusation Emerges

The accusation surfaced as if on cue with malevolent intent, casting a dark shadow over the selfless act that had once been praised. It was a jolting moment where whispered words twisted generosity into greed and distorted self-sacrifice into self-serving deceit. Imagine the chill that runs down the spine as charity is smeared with lies, the stew of confusion it brews in the hearts of those who had seen nothing but goodwill. This insidious turn, brothers and sisters in faith, isn't just a stroke of misfortune; it is a calculated snare set by the adversary, known for masquerading as an angel of light, seeking to destroy reputations and dilute the essence of the Gospel through division and suspicion. It is a vivid reminder that we must wear the whole armour of God, for our struggle is not against flesh and blood, and even in our most benevolent moments, we're walking through a battlefield, unseen yet as accurate as the warmth of the sun, as cold as the accusation that now stands before us.

The Agony of Misunderstood Intentions

We've ventured through the various tactics employed by our adversary, the creeping subtleties he injects into our lives, weaving his webs of temptation and accusation. But perhaps one of the most heart-wrenching ordeals arises when our intentions, pure and well meaning are woefully misinterpreted, tainting the essence of our generosity and leaving us in a desolate place of misunderstanding. It is a peculiar agony, misjudged intentions. It gnaws at the soul because it strikes at the heart of who we are, and that's love. We're vulnerable when we reach out, showing God's love to others—through guidance or companionship. And it is in this vulnerability where Satan often likes to strike, twisting feelings and planting seeds of doubt.

Consider the shepherd who offers his cloak against the biting cold to a traveller, only to be accused of leaving another in the frost. As selfless as it may have been, the action is viewed through a distorted lens, leading to accusations and discontent amongst the flock he so dearly tends. This is the enemy's tactic: to distort and destroy from within. Our intentions can be misunderstood in myriad ways. A complement taken as condescension, an offer of help seen as meddling, or viewed as interference. In these instances, the pain is tangible because, at our core, we meant well. And when these good intentions are put through distortion, it can feel like we're wrestling against forces unseen. It is this misunderstanding that can breed isolation. One begins to question oneself: Am I the source of the problem. Self-doubt creeps in, and the enemy's whispers become torrents of confusion. 'Was it wrong to help?' Should I have stayed out of it? These are not questions of our making but of an orchestration designed to disrupt and dishearten.

The agony intensifies when our actions are questioned by those we hold dear: the church community, fellow believers, and perhaps most painful, those we have set out to serve. It is a trial by fire where our faith is both the accused and the source of our strength. In such a quagmire, we must cling to the truth that our God is a God of clarity, not confusion. When misunderstood, emulating Christ becomes our solace; after all, He was without sin but bore all accusations. Through His example, we must navigate these troubled waters—forgiving those who misunderstand us and loving them still. The path forward is not to recoil in the face of misunderstanding but to go ahead with wisdom and caution. We must temper our generosity with discernment, and while we cannot control the beliefs of others, we can control our response to their misinterpretations.

Take solace in the fact that this is not a unique trial. The Bible is replete with tales of misunderstood, mistreated, and maligned people despite their noble intentions. His brothers sold Joseph (Gen. 37:12-36), David fled King Saul's unwarranted wrath (1 Sam. 21ff), and Daniel faced the lions' den (Dan. 6: 10-23). Yet they stood steadfast, trusting in the Lord. The heartache from intentions turned upside down is a heavy cross to bear. It requires a depth of faith and a reservoir of grace. In times of such distress, the community plays a crucial role.

Surrounding one's self with fellow believers, seeking their counsel, and allowing their support to bolster our weakened spirits is vital.

This is a storm that will pass. Remember, our Lord calms storms. Clinging to this hope, this truth that He will still every wave and silence every wind, is essential. This agony of misunderstood intentions is one chapter in our walk of faith.

Throughout our trials, we are called to keep a posture of humility. We shall use these experiences to reflect on our actions and examine our hearts. It is not entirely about whether our intentions were misunderstood but whether our hearts are aligned with God's will. As we walk this road of uncertainty, we refine our trust in Him, knowing He sees both intention and outcome. And in the depths of our struggle, we must remember to guard our own hearts, lest we, too, misinterpret the actions of others. In doing so, we insulate the body of Christ from similar attacks, for unity is our most excellent defence against the adversary's divisive strategies. We are not only receivers of grace but also dispensers of it.

Hold fast and stand firm for those caught in misunderstood intentions. It is a testing of your faith, purifying it like gold. Through this fire, your commitment to Christ's love and your resilience in God's faithfulness will shine brightly, a reflection of His abiding presence even in the agony of misunderstood intentions.

Chapter Five

The Trial of False Witness

As the narrative unfolds, the harsh glare of the courtroom intensifies, exposing the jagged edges of a spiritual battlefield where truth clashes with deception. The heart of the accused pounds with a mix of fear and prayer, casting mental pleas heavenward while the voice of the false witness resonates, echoing off the walls like a sinister melody. Squaring one's shoulders and rebutting the lies takes more than a firm stance; it beckons for the whole armour of God, a truth grounded deeply in Scripture, unwavering and polished by the trials faced.

This chapter isn't about falling prey to despair, but rather, standing tall and understanding that Satan's whispers find volume through human vessels, misguided and used as pawns to brew discord and tarnish testimonies. It is about recognising that even Christ, in His perfection, faced accusers, and thus, in our following of Him, we might too. The righteous may wobble, but don't fall when anchored in faith. Though daunting, the trial of false witness serves as a forge for character and a testament to unwavering trust in divine justice over human judgement.

Confronting the Allegations

In the charged atmosphere of the trial, where whispers of treachery hung heavy, came the moment to face the allegations. It was a crucible that tested the soul, demanding strength and wisdom in the face of cunning deceit. Those standing accused knew too well the vicious sting of a lying tongue, a scenario not unfamiliar to the narrative woven through the Scriptures, where the most upright hearts encountered trials shaped by the deceiver's hand. With every fabric of their being, they had to muster the courage to stare down the falsehoods, armed with nothing but their unwavering conviction and an acute awareness of the spiritual warfare that raged unseen. Their response was not solely for their own sake but also to illuminate the truth for those watching with bated breath. After all, wasn't it the truth that would set them free? In that courtroom, the reality wasn't just a set of facts to be argued but a testament to the faith that held them unshaken amidst the tempest of false witness.

The Emotional Toll of Injustice
In the earlier sections, we've explored the precipice of false accusations and their ability to ensnare even the most faithful servants. Let us delve into how such injustices can gnaw at our spirits, causing emotional turmoil. The acknowledgement of this suffering is not to wallow in despair but to understand the battle against us—a struggle not of flesh and blood but of spiritual realms playing out in our minds and hearts. Injustice, mainly when born out of malicious intent, behaves as a thief in the night. It is not the loss of material possessions that afflicts us most but the theft of our peace, trust in others, and the warmth of relationships.

When a pastor, walking the path of righteousness, faces the poison of false witness, their world shakes. Suddenly, the comfort once drawn from their congregation and community can be replaced with the stinging chill of isolation. Faced with such adversity, it is human to question one's actions — where did I falter? The heart, tender and worn from serving tirelessly, now must defend its intent and purity. The soul wrestles with the shadow of doubt, a spectre ushered in by the enemy to weaken resolve. The enemy doesn't only wish to see the believer fall but to flounder in the mire of confusion and pain along the way. Disbelief and shock may be the first companions of the accused, followed closely by an ache in the marrow of their bones — anguish. It burrows deep, unsettling the once firm confidence foundation in self and divine providence. It is not just a personal sorrow; it is mourning over the tarnish of one's witness for Christ. After all, how can one lead effectively when cloaked in the pall of an untruth?

The relentless barrage of false allegations can cause a persistent sense of unrest. Sleep eludes, anxiety takes residence, and the leader's once steady hands are now tremulous. Here, it becomes clear that the enemy is assailing the individual and the church's broader mission—to halt the spreading of the Gospel that thrives on trust, compassion, and integrity. Bitterness can seep into the heart like a slow poison. It can sour the well of forgiveness, a well that the servant of the Lord must draw from often. And, should bitterness take root, it strains the believers' reflection of Christ, who forgave even those who pinned Him on a cross.

Thus, the trial is not only external. Within, a tempest rages — a spiritual struggle to hold onto grace. Amid the storm, despair can become a shadowy figure lurking behind every failed attempt to clear one's name. It whispers the futility of fighting back, urging the wronged to surrender to the label of outcast. Yet, we're reminded in this darkness that Christ was acquainted with undeserved suffering. His example encourages us to carry our cross, knowing that our vindication rests in the hands of the Almighty.

Frustration often joins the ensemble of emotions when the usual channels of justice seem clogged with misunderstanding or apathy. A righteous anger may flare, directed towards the systems that are supposed to protect the innocent but sometimes fail. The servant of the Lord must navigate this, balancing the God-given desire for justice with the command to keep a spirit not given to vengeance.

Loneliness, too, rears its head, for the accused often finds that their support network dwindles or becomes fickle as gossip and speculation build. In whom can they confide? Who will stand by them when their reputation is stained? Every departure magnifies the feeling of betrayal, yet within this solitude, the victim may learn the depth of their reliance on God.

Hopelessness can become a spectre at the feast of faith. When every effort to clear one's name seems ineffective, when prayers for deliverance appear to go unanswered, the sense of abandonment can be overwhelming. Remember, though, that the Lord's timing is not our own, and it is in the waiting that we often meet God's refining process, trimming away all that is not of Him and strengthening our dependence on His saving grace. Injustice scars not just the psyche but also the soul. It isn't a surface wound; it is a deep tear in one's identity as a child of God. Such experiences force us into Gethsemane to grapple with our own will versus the will of the Father, to kneel in the garden and surrender our battered hearts to His care—a care that promises new life through tribulation.

However, amid such trials, a peculiar beauty can appear—the beauty of shared suffering. It is in our brokenness that the body of Christ is often most vividly realised. As one member suffers, others rally, creating bonds fused in the fire of adversity. These relationships reflect the love of Jesus, a fierce, sacrificial, and unyielding love in the face of the oppressor.

Let us always remember our ultimate victory through Christ. Injustice, while it can tear at the fabric of our beings, is but a momentary affliction considering eternity. The cross that looms large and burdensome is borne not in our strength but through the enduring power of the Holy Spirit. Resurrection hope is our foundation, even when the world seems against us. So, although the emotional toll of injustice can be harrowing, leaving us feeling battered and bruised, we are called to rise each day with our armour in place. Truth, righteousness, readiness grounded in the Gospel of peace, faith as a shield, salvation as a helmet, and the word of God as our sword—fully equipped to withstand the devil's wiles (Eph.6:10-18). Consider this, my friends, as a clarion call to resilience. Persevere, not because you are unscathed, but because He who is in you is greater than he who is in the world (1 John 4:4).

May we face the emotional toll of injustice not as victims but as victors; not scarred but sculpted, refined like gold through the furnace, ready to shine once more for His glory?

Chapter Six

Clinging to Faith Amidst the Storm

Here we stand in the tempest of trials, where the winds of accusation howl and the waves of doubt rise menacingly clinging to faith amidst the storm. Isn't it easy to give in to despondency when the skies of our lives are overcast, and relentless rains threaten to drown our spirits? Yet, this chapter invites you to plant your feet firmly on the Rock, even as the tempest rages. We'll explore the profound resilience rooted in unwavering faith, the kind that the world doesn't quite comprehend.

Engaging in fervent prayer becomes our lifeline, the heart-to-heart communion with our Creator that anchors us. And let us not forget the strength found in the fellowship of believers—a community that holds fast together, reinforcing each other's faith when one falters. They say there's a silver lining in every storm cloud, and perhaps, just perhaps, our trials are that bleak backdrop against which the brilliance of faith shines ever so brightly, guiding us to stand firm in our beliefs, come what may.

Standing Firm in Beliefs

In the cacophony of accusations and trials, it is easy to waver, to let the fierce winds of adversity chip away at our spiritual bedrock. But let us stir up that resolute Spirit within, which firmly grips our core convictions. We're reminded that it is not mere human resilience but a divine anchor that holds us steady. Our faith isn't a wispy cloud that drifts with the day's troubles—it is more akin to a deeply rooted tree, steadfast amidst the howling storm.

Standing firm in our beliefs doesn't dismiss the reality of our struggles; it is an act of defiance against the doubts that seek to entangle our hearts. Remember, it isn't our strength on which we lean but the unyielding truth of God's Word. And in the moments when your knees wobble and your heart quakes, that's precisely when your faith, the evidence of things unseen, becomes your bulwark against surrender. So, let us lock our spiritual armour in place, engage with the shield of faith and wield the sword of the Spirit, for the battles we face, though fierce, cannot overcome the power bestowed upon us from on high.

The Role of Prayer and Community

After delving into the intricate web Satan weaves to ensnare the unwary, we must turn to the lifelines that help us stay afloat in these tempestuous times. Prayer and community aren't just lovely additions to a Christian's life; they are, in so many ways, the frontline defence against the deceiver's schemes. When the darkness of false accusations and misunderstandings looms, it is easy to feel isolated—like a lone warrior facing an army.

But let us not forget that we've been blessed with the gift of prayer, an open line of communication with the Almighty, and an ever-present help in times of need. Through prayer, we find the strength to withstand the enemy's wiles, for it centres and reconnects us with the Lord's unchanging truth. Yet, prayer isn't just an individual refuge. When we unite in prayer as a community, we forge a stronger bond than any ploy the devil can conjure. There's an unspoken power in believers' collective will and faith, gathering to intercede for one another. The early church showed us this strength—gathering in homes, sharing meals, and lifting their voices in prayer together. They knew that together their prayers had the power to shake foundations.

In times of trial, such as the distress of an accused pastor or Christian, the community serves as a testament to God's unending grace. Other Christians rally around the afflicted, encircling them with the love and support that reflects Christ's compassion. To stand in solidarity with a Christian brother or sister, to carry their burdens, is a clear commandment from the Scriptures. Look around; the people you worship with aren't just fellow churchgoers. They're your family in Christ, ready to stand by you when the storms hit.

Remember to appreciate the resources we have in each other. The enemy delights in division and discord among believers, for a divided house cannot stand. But when we unite, setting aside our differences to focus on the spiritual battle, we can rely on God's promise that where two or three gather in His name, He will be also. Brushing against the grain of individualism that pervades our western culture, the Christian doctrine celebrates community. In the context of a pastor or Christian wrongfully accused, this bond of fellowship becomes increasingly essential. The community that prays together declares an unspoken yet powerful statement that they will not be swayed by unfounded allegations or an attempt by Satan to tarnish a fellow child of God.

While praying for the pastor's strength and vindication, the community becomes a beacon of forgiveness and grace. Extending grace is difficult, especially when the accusations fly and the crowd leans towards judgment. Yet, this is precisely what Jesus did during His ministry. Facing down the allegations hurled at Him, He chose to love, forgive, and pray even for those who looked to bring Him harm. This radical call to love underlines the need for prayer partnerships when darkness tries to prevail. And Satan, who aims to distort and destroy, finds himself powerless against love in its most accurate form.

So, when we stand together with fellow Christians and pray for those who persecute us, we're wielding a weapon that pierces through the shadows. In the fabric of fellowship, it is equally essential for Christians to be discerning. Sound biblical teaching and communal wisdom can help in navigating through deceitful situations. Awareness of Satan's strategies is crucial but recognising that not every accusation may be a direct attack from the enemy also matters. Wisdom calls for truth to prevail, patience in judgment, and love to guide our reactions.

Moreover, let us remember the importance of intercession. We're instructed to pray for all people, leaders included, so that we may live peaceful and quiet lives in all godliness and holiness. Therefore, while supporting a Christian or a servant of God in tribulation, the congregation's prayers can also encompass the wider community, authorities, and even the accuser. The heart of the gospel is to bring reconciliation, not just vindication. A pastor's ordeal can also serve as a crucial learning curve for the congregation. It can be a poignant reminder of our vulnerability to sin and Satan's tactics.

The community's response, rooted in prayer and unity, can show the watching world that faith is not quickly shattered even in dire circumstances. Let us not allow Satan to have a foothold in our spiritual family. What's needed is vigilance in prayer and an unwavering commitment to one another. Just as Paul encouraged the Ephesians to wear the whole armour of God, so too must we equip ourselves, supporting our leaders and enveloping them in prayer. This is how we fight the good fight of faith. This is how we stand against the devil's schemes.

Community, therefore, isn't a mere social club; it embodies the living Christ among us—a fortress against the snares of malice and a garden where the fruits of the Spirit can flourish even when adversity strikes. And so, as we stand shoulder to shoulder, let us remember that the battle is not against flesh and blood but against rulers, against authorities, against the powers of this dark world. Our joined hands and hearts in prayer form a barrier Satan cannot breach. We are stronger together, united in Christ, resilient in the face of trials. This is the role of prayer and community in the life of a believer, and it shines brightest when tested by the trials conceived in the depths of the enemy's lair.

Chapter Seven

Navigating the Legal Labyrinth

The road needed to be straight and the journey predictable. Still, as we found ourselves ensconced in the twists and turns of the legal maze, it became crystal clear that there's a spiritual dimension to every earthly struggle—even in the cold, hard benches of human courts and churches' disciplinary panels. Embroiling oneself in legal proceedings is no walk in the park, especially when innocence is clothed in guilt. Here, one's integrity can come under relentless attack, and the system that's designed to uphold justice, oddly enough, sometimes ends up feeling like a labyrinth designed by the enemy himself.

So, how do we navigate such treacherous paths where every step could be a trap? It requires tenacity, wisdom beyond our keenest legal acumen, and an unwavering trust that He who is just shall not forsake His beloved. To weather the storm within the courts or disciplinary committees, we're going to delve into a Christ-centred strategy formed not just by the letter of the law but by the Spirit, who equips us with the whole armour of God to stand against the wiles lurking in the labyrinth of legalese.

The Pastor's Defence

As we delve into the intricacies of legal challenges that religious leaders might face, we can't dismiss the vital importance of a well-articulated defence. Against the backdrop of a society quick to accuse, Christians need to equip themselves with the truth, sharpened by the wisdom of the Holy Spirit. They, including Pastors, must stand with integrity in this treacherous terrain where accusations might fly like fiery darts, ensuring that every rebuttal is anchored in righteousness and delivered with a Christ-like composure. It is not merely a matter of legal savvy; it is about manifesting the fruits of the Spirit even in the most pressure-laden courtrooms. Their defence isn't just for their sake but a testimony to their flock, demonstrating how to wield faith as a shield, even as they navigate the thorny thicket of the justice system, including churches' appointed disciplinary committees. Let us consider Pastor's experience in his discipline hearing here.

Thom sat in disbelief as he read his fellow ministers' reports. They were filled with inaccuracies and seemed to paint him negatively. He couldn't understand why they would want to make him look guilty. He had never seen the reports before they were submitted, so he couldn't suggest corrections. As he faced the church disciplinary panel, he couldn't believe how they treated him. He had served faithfully for thirty years without a single complaint, yet they acted as if it meant nothing. Both he and Mrs. Johnson had legal representation, but Thom had naively assumed that in a Christian environment, the truth would prevail. But as the proceedings went on, it became clear that the representative for the accuser was not interested in the truth.

They were simply looking to convict Thom. Mrs Johnson had even requested a screen to avoid eye contact with him, and his family wasn't allowed to be present to hear her testimony. Thom's family had welcomed Mrs Johnson into their lives, and her unfounded accusations were unfathomable to them. Despite Thom providing written evidence from all the churches he had ministered in over the years, the panel, consisting of three ordained ministers and one lay member, couldn't see through her lies.

To make matters worse, the church had failed to remind Mrs Johnson that she was not allowed to habitually level accusations against other Christians without witnesses or evidence from the teachings of scripture. As the hearing ended, Thom couldn't help but feel betrayed by those he had considered his colleagues and friends. He had always believed in the church's power to do what was right and just but now he realised that even in a place of faith, there could still be injustice and deceit. But he held onto his faith, knowing that the truth would prevail and justice would be served.

Legal Obstacles and Triumphs

It is been quite the journey, navigating the complexities of a legal system that seems blind to the spiritual underpinnings of our struggles. As Christians, we're called to fight battles not of this world, but sometimes, the battles choose us, and they manifest in courts with gavels and decrees. There's something inherently gut wrenching about seeing a pastor, an anointed leader, ensnared by legal shackles, especially when the intentions behind their actions were pure.

However, we must understand that these legal battles are not mere coincidences or strokes of ill fortune. They're often the result of the enemy's strategy, calculated moves engineered to disrupt and discredit the work of those who strive to uphold righteousness. Our adversary enjoys watching as we're dragged through the mud of legalities because it distracts and discredits, tarnishing reputations and sowing seeds of doubt among the faithful.

The tale of the trials we face in courtrooms mirrors the broader struggle against a malevolent force that yearns to distort justice. Legal obstacles often come in the form of convoluted laws, red tape, and the unfortunate truth that the legal system is sometimes manipulated to favour those with ill intent over the innocent. A pastor's life, devoted to service and sacrifice, can be quickly overshadowed by allegations and lawsuits, whether justified or not.

These legal skirmishes can seem daunting. Paperwork forms a mountain range, legal terms become a confusing babble, and one's Spirit dwindles under the cold fluorescence of legal offices. Yet, these trials can also lead to triumphs that serve as unequivocal testaments to the divine hand still at work in our world. As believers, we must cling to the scripture's promise that no weapon formed against us shall prosper. It is a promise that extends beyond the physical and spiritual into the institutional. In every instance where a servant of God has been falsely accused, their integrity impugned by twisted words and deceit, there have been awe-inspiring stories of vindication.

Legal victories that seemed impossible appear, and prophecies are fulfilled through the verdicts of earthly judges. These aren't mere coincidences but the spoils of faith-fuelled warfare, securing a powerful narrative of God's deliverance against a backdrop of human governance.

The faith community plays an irreplaceable role in such victories. When one of their flocks faces the gavel of judgment, collective prayers rise like incense, and spiritual support becomes tangible. Legal defence funds are gathered, skilled Christian lawyers step forward, and the community girds their loins with the belt of truth. Yet, there are moments when the triumph isn't immediate. Days turn into weeks, weeks into months, and sometimes, even years. Hope wavers as the legal system grinds on with the slow grind of justice delayed. But we must not interpret the delay as defeat. Through perseverance in faith and unwavering trust in the Lord's timing, many have seen the dawn break on their night of legal turmoil. Data doesn't lie; stats have unfurled stories of pastors and Christians who've walked free, exonerated from charges that once loomed like a judge's gavel over their heads. It is also sparked a fresh understanding within the church of the importance of due diligence, of constructing boundaries that shelter from such legal snares.

Our legal triumphs serve as glorious evidence to a watching world that truth prevails, that light pierces through the most impenetrable darkness. We must dare to believe that our God is an advocate who pleads on our behalf, even in the courtrooms of this world. Each victory restores the fallen and serves as a beacon to those still navigating the shadowy valleys of legal battles. Rest assured, the enemy may be shrewd in his tactics, yet he needs to be more omniscient. While he may manipulate circumstances and weave webs of deception within the legal domain, he cannot contend with the Spirit of truth.

Our most excellent legal strategist lives not in the law firms but in the heavenly realms. And let us talk about those who champion our cause in the courtrooms. Christian legal advocates who arm themselves with the whole armour of God are unsung heroes in these narratives. They delve into statute books with prayers on their lips, employing earthly knowledge and divine wisdom to stand against the schemes of the wicked.

The church must view these legal issues not as mere inconveniences but as accurate battlegrounds where the spiritual and temporal intersect. Whether it is property disputes, accusations against church leaders, or religious liberty cases, each legal encounter has implications for the broader Body of Christ. Yet, in these battles, we're reminded of our calling to be as shrewd as serpents and as innocent as doves. You see, spiritual warfare requires sagacity and discernment, and sometimes, that means engaging with worldly systems with godly wisdom to defend the defenceless, to advocate for truth and to navigate through accusations and legal traps set by those who do not wish us well.

Satan's schemes may seem overwhelming, and the legal landscape sometimes feels rigged against the righteous. But let us lift our eyes to the hills, to the Judge who reigns above all judges. Every legal obstacle overcome, each surprising triumph is a resounding gavel of God's verdict: He is for us, and with Him, victory is assured. In conclusion, never underestimate the power of steadfast, prayerful endurance in the face of legal adversity.

The courtroom may appear to be the devil's playground, but it is a stage for God's glory to manifest, for faith to be fortified, for the righteous to be raised up, and for justice, divine justice, ultimately to prevail.

Chapter Eight

The Church's Reaction to Scandal

In the tempest of scandal, the church's response either forges a path to redemption or lets the storm shipwreck the faith of many. Leaders and congregants stand at a crossroads when whispers of wrongdoing grow into a roar. Will they succumb to the spread of distrust and betrayal or rise above, unified in Christ's love and grace? To navigate such treacherous waters, keeping unity is not just ideal but critical. It is about more than just managing appearances or damage control. It is about embodying the very essence of the gospel—forgiveness, restoration, and truth — while rejecting the lure of judgment and division that Satan so cleverly dangles. The church must rally in arms, protecting the wounded, seeking the whole story, and refusing to let a house built on rock crumble over the sand of speculation and hearsay.

Maintaining Unity

In the throes of scandal, when the murmurs of discord threaten to splinter our congregation, we're reminded that unity isn't merely a high-minded ideal but the lifeblood of our faith community. As tensions mount and sides begin to form, our focus must shift to reconciliation and fortifying our collective bond in Christ. During these trying moments, we must lean heavily on the wisdom laid out in Scripture, embracing forgiveness and exercising patience with one another, all the while mindful that discord is a foothold for the adversary's influence.

It is essential, then, not to let differences ferment into division but to use this to prove the transformative power of God's love in uniting us fostering peace and understanding in the very face of turmoil. The task isn't light, yet within these challenges, our unity reflects the potent hope we hold— a testament to the world of His grace at work in us.

Handling Dissension Within the Flock

Any seasoned shepherd knows that tending to a flock can be more taxing than herding the sheep through rocky pastures. There's an art to it, an attentiveness that spots the first signs of disturbance and homes in with wisdom and care. In the heart of a church family, discord can manifest and, like a silent disease, spread quickly, sowing seeds of division. We can't be naive to think Satan's fingers aren't in this pie, using disagreements and strife to weaken the body of believers.

Sadly, it is not uncommon for bad blood to emerge within congregations. One accusing glance or whispered rumour can ignite the fire that seems impossible to quench. Yet, we've got to recall the pivotal role of leadership in these scenarios. The pastor and every mature Christian play a crucial role in navigating these tricky waters, ensuring the ship doesn't capsize under the weight of growing contention.

Let us face it—unfortunately, the enemy's tactics are effective. He's a master of exploiting vulnerabilities, causing Christians who once stood side by side in worship to draw lines in the sand. The challenge then lies in approaching these tense situations not with a heart eager for confrontation but with a spirit seeking reconciliation and peace. Do we recall the Apostle Paul's guidance to the Corinthians amidst their disputes? He didn't scold them from a lofty pedestal but addressed each concern with grace and a deep longing for unity. Like Paul, church leaders today must embody that delicate blend of firmness and gentleness when faced with internal dissension.

Empathy is key. Walking a mile in someone else's shoes isn't just an aged adage; it is divine counsel for peacemaking. As leaders, we must listen—really listen—to the grievances of each party. Understanding their perspective allows us to mediate effectively, finding common ground that often appears buried beneath the turmoil.

However, it isn't solely a pastor's job to handle these bitter moments. The entire church body must be alert, ready to usher in words of life rather than fuel the fires of dispute. It is about being peacemakers who 'blessed are the peacemakers,' as beautifully stated in the Beatitudes. What about discipline, though? Some might call for stringent action, drawing lines and setting examples. There's certainly a place for biblical discipline, but it must always be administered with a view towards restoration rather than punishment.

Prayers, patience, and private discussions are often the first tools of choice long before public measures are considered. Forgiveness is the cornerstone here. Let us not forget the parable of the unmerciful servant who, though forgiven much, refused to forgive a little (Matt. 18:23-35). Holding onto grudges goes against the very fabric of the gospel. It is a painful process to forgive and extend grace, but it is what we're called to do, following the lead of one who forgave us much more. Transparency within leadership is also potent in healing rifts. When leaders show openness about their fallibility, it can soften hearts and encourage a more forgiving attitude throughout the congregation. The pastor shouldn't stand aloof but be part of the flock, showing that they, too, rely on the grace they preach.

Moreover, preventive teaching should be a regular staple in the spiritual diet of the church. The Wisdom of Solomon comes to mind, suggesting that a house divided against itself cannot stand. Teaching unity, understanding the body of Christ, and promoting healthy communication are not just optional extras; they form the bedrock of a robust and resilient church. Let us also harness the power of prayer in these situations. The early church was found on its knees amidst persecution

How much more should we be found there when the threat comes from within? Prayer unifies and strengthens, invoking the power of the God of peace to preside over disputes.

As for the flock, each member has a role too. The power of a united body is to be considered. When each person looks to build rather than criticise, support rather than isolate, that's when you see God knitting his people back together. Nevertheless, it is crucial to recognise that some conflicts are deep-rooted and require more than a quick chat to put things right. In such cases, the wisdom of bringing in a neutral, mature believer to counsel might be needed. This guidance from outside the immediate situation can bridge gaps and begin the journey towards healing.

There might be moments when, despite every effort, reconciliation appears out of reach. Even then, it is paramount to maintain a posture of hope and grace. It shows the community that, 1although we stumble and struggle, our dedication to living out the gospel message is still unshaken.

In closing, taking on dissension within the church is no light task, but it can't be sidestepped. We must meet it head-on, armed with love, wisdom, and the Word of God, as testimonies to the world of His unifying power. In unity, we reflect the true nature of God's kingdom, and in doing so, we foil one of Satan's most devious ploys against His church.

Chapter Nine

The Lessons of Job Revisited

As we turn our gaze back to the enduring trials of Job, we can't help but unearth the rich seams of insight that affirm our current struggle against the snares of Satan. The ancient narrative speaks directly to our hearts, whispering the virtues of patience and the profound peace in divine wisdom—even when besieged by the harshest trials.

We're reminded that afflictions, however fierce, can serve as the kiln in which our faith is not only tested but also, strikingly, solidified. The plight of Job is our silent teacher, insistently urging us not to cast our gaze on the immediate maelstrom of hardship but to anchor our souls in the steadfast promise of God's sovereignty. Job, a wealthy, blameless and upright man, experiences immense suffering through losing his wealth, children, and health. He wrestles with the illogical nature of his suffering and seeks answers from his friends and, ultimately, from God. Job's friends, Eliphaz, Bildad, and Zophar, represent conventional wisdom, believing that suffering is a direct result of sin and that Job must have done something to deserve his plight. However, as the narrative unfolds, it becomes clear that Job's suffering is not due to his sin or lack of piety, challenging the common belief that suffering is a direct punishment for wrongdoing.

The book suggests that suffering can be a part of God's mysterious plan and that there may be reasons beyond our understanding for allowing it. God's response to Job's questions in the book also suggests that human beings cannot comprehend the entirety of God's purposes and plans. This biblical insight teaches us humility and the need to acknowledge our human limitations in understanding the mind of God.

The book also raises serious questions about God's justice and righteousness, as Job argues that his suffering is undeserved and calls for God to justify himself. The book does not provide a simple answer to the evil problem; it somewhat complicates the issue and invites deeper contemplation.

In Job's dialogues with his friends and his lamentations before God, we see a raw and honest exploration of the human experience of suffering. He expresses deep anguish, despair, and frustration, highlighting the emotional and psychological dimensions of suffering. One takeaway from this theological insight is that Christians can and should wrestle with God and engage in honest dialogue during grief. However, it challenges the notion that human wisdom and understanding are sufficient to comprehend the mysteries of God. Job's friends, who initially offer explanations for his suffering, are ultimately silenced by God's response, emphasizing the limitations of our wisdom and the unfathomable nature of divine providence.

Job ultimately accepts God's wisdom. He is rewarded and his fortunes are restored. Let us, then, embrace the essence of Job's unyielding endurance, learning anew that even when our generosity seems to breed contempt and our intentions are twisted against us, a higher throne oversees the ultimate reckoning of all deeds under heaven.

Patience and Endurance in Suffering

As we journey deeper into the heart of Job's narrative, we confront one of life's most gruelling challenges—staying steadfast under relentless suffering. It is a path littered with silence and storm, where every whisper of hope dissipates with the howling winds of hardship. Yet, in this crucible, our character is tested and fortified. We're invited, not to a blind resignation, but to a fierce tenacity that grips onto faith even when every sign points to its abandonment.

The story of Job isn't a tale of passive acceptance. It is a gritty saga of enduring the agony with a tenacious hold on the divine tapestry we're part of yet can't fully comprehend. The journey isn't marked by a stoic detachment but by a vulnerable, raw, almost seismic dependence on God, who remains unshaken when everything else trembles. So, when we find ourselves locked in the vice of tribulation, let us remember that it is not the absence of immediate deliverance that defines our story but the persistent, dogged resolve to trust in the unwavering faithfulness of God amidst suffering. In this space, patience isn't merely waiting; it is active engagement with the belief that our current page is not where the story ends.

Finding Peace in Divine Wisdom
In the impassioned whirl of life's unexpected tempests, where the din of chaos threatens to overwhelm the soul, we're reminded to seek refuge in something greater than ourselves. Solace — profound and transformational — is found in the bosom of divine wisdom. This wisdom isn't just a treasure trove of intellectual insights but a wellspring of peace that surpasses all understanding, available for those willing to drink from its serene depths. The Scriptures hold the key to unlocking this sublime peace. It can often be tempting to rely solely on our understanding. Yet, there's a marked difference between human insight and the divine perspective. God's wisdom calls for an abandonment of the ego and a wholehearted trust in His sovereign guidance.

The book of James remarks that if we lack wisdom, we should ask God, who gives generously to all without finding fault, and it will be given to us. Let us take a moment to ponder the narrative of Job, a man bedecked in manifold sorrows yet steadfast in his pursuit of God's wisdom. Job's tale isn't merely one of suffering; it epitomises finding peace amid life's savage storms. How often do we, like Job, find ourselves stripped of the familiar, grappling with enigmas beyond our understanding? And yet, Job's unwavering faith in God's wisdom and resolve to eschew bitterness crowns his journey with peace.

Truly, discernment lies not in the mastery of theological intricacies but in the simple, humble alignment with God's Word and will. The psalmist beautifully articulates it as the fear of the Lord, saying that it is the beginning of wisdom. This fear isn't the cringing dread of a malevolent deity but rather a reverent awe of the Almighty, the Creator, Lover, and Sustainer of all life. During trials, it is crucial to remember that while Satan may intend to dismantle our faith through sly mechanisms and devastating blows, God's providence remoulds what's broken, guiding us towards a horizon filled with hope and reclamation.

When we teeter on the brink of despair, divine wisdom whispers to us, urging us to look beyond the transient and perceive the eternal. Christians should strive to emulate Christ's reliance on Scripture for wisdom and guidance. In instances of temptation or accusation, He countered with the Word, for it was the well from which He drew His strength and resolve. Just as Christ rested in his Father's wisdom, so must we learn to rest assured of God's flawless plans for us.

It is also important not to misconstrue the role of suffering in the Christian walk. Suffering isn't an aberration to be shunned at all costs but can be an instrument of God's wisdom. Remember, our Saviour himself was no stranger to pain.

In this light, our tribulations can be a crucible for character, a gateway to more profound wisdom, moulding our spirits into a closer semblance of Christ. This reliance on divine wisdom doesn't render us passive but steels our resolve. It gives us the clarity to discern manipulations of the wicked and the fortitude to withstand them. God's Word is often likened to armour, equipping us to stand firm against the deceptions of the evil one. In it, we find the grounding truths that hold us steady amidst life's upheaval. Yet, divine wisdom isn't merely for the towering crises of life; it is equally pertinent in the mundane. In every juncture where choice beckons, this celestial guidance can illuminate our path, helping us to navigate with integrity and grace. Quick fixes and shortcuts hold no allure when our charts are set by the reliable compass of God's wisdom.

Moreover, divine wisdom fosters unity within the church. It anchors us to a standard foundation, helping to avoid the pitfalls of discord and misunderstanding. As Paul admonishes, let us not be wise in our own eyes but agree towards one another, deferring to the wisdom from above that is first pure, then peaceable, gentle, and easy to be entreated. In our quest for peace, we must cultivate the discipline of listening — a heart posture attuned not to the clamour of our anxieties but to the still, small voice of God.

In the quietude of prayer and reflection, we often hear the profound echoes of divine wisdom shaping our convictions and soothing our restlessness. Lastly, peace blossoms in the community garden, where collective wisdom often dwarfs individual insight. The early church thrived on mutual edification and wise counsel amongst believers, setting a precedent for us to follow. Leaning on one another, undergirded by prayer, we refresh our spirits in the brooks of fellowship and collective wisdom.

As we continue to stand vigilant against the wiles of Satan, let us do so armed with divine wisdom that weaves through our beings like a golden thread. Herein lies our peace — not in the cessation of storms but in the knowing, deep in our marrow, that He who calms the tempest is steering our course. So, in every moment of doubt, when voices of discord and malignance swarm around us, may we fix our gaze firmly on Him. Let us seek wisdom in His presence, where clarity dawns and peace descend like a gentle dove. In embracing God's divine wisdom, we find an unassailable refuge from the schemes that look to entangle and embitter our souls. As believers, let us then walk in tranquillity, cradled in the assurance that the depths of God's understanding know no bounds and, in His wisdom, there is rest for the weary, hope for the disheartened, and undisturbed peace for the besieged heart.

Chapter Ten

The Long Road to Vindication

Ah, the winding path of clearing one's name—it is fraught with potholes that'll jolt even the sturdiest of faith-laden vehicles. Nonetheless, it is a journey many must tread, heels dug deep into the soil of perseverance. As we wander this track, flanked by tall grasses of despair and brambles of doubt, let us grasp tightly the soothing balm of patience. The clock ticks hardly to the rhythm of our hearts, but it is important to remember that justice, though often tardy, tends not to forsake its date with the righteous. It is about hunkering in the trenches of endurance while armed with a shield of truth and a sword of the Spirit, knowing that every step forward is a stride in the grand embroidery of His plan.

We embark on the road to vindication, leaning on the robust pillars of faith—that compass which orients us towards hope, even when the horizon seems cloaked in the dusk of our trials.

Awaiting Justice
Within the sanctuary of faith's embrace, the path to vindication weaves through a thicket of trials, a poignant reflection of the spiritual battlefield upon which we stand. As the afflicted wait, cloaked in the armour of steadfast belief, the clamour for justice echoes in the chambers of their hearts. In these quiet moments of anticipation, the soul, braced by prayer, lingers on the cusp of deliverance, yearning for the balance of scales tipped by deceit.

The hours turn into days and patience can wear thin, yet each tick of the clock is a reminder that the Author of Time pens a story more extensive than what the eye can see. For the faithful caught in this maelstrom, the wait isn't merely a test of endurance but a silent sermon on the sovereignty of the 'Most High God', who assures that all will be called into account under His watchful gaze.

The Power of Forgiveness in Healing

I want to explore forgiveness's profound impact on our healing journey. Isn't it remarkable how forgiveness can often feel like a heavy burden lifted from the chest? Forgiveness is like a balm for the wounded soul in a world fraught with conflict and hurt. Let us consider its role, especially when the darkness seems to press in from all sides.

Imagine the scene: Pastor Thom, Christian leader, swathed in the shadow of false accusations, stands broken before the discipline panel. The sting of betrayal is raw, and the pathway to vindication is long and arduous. Yet, during his suffering, a beacon of hope appears – forgiveness. Some may think it is easier said than done, and they're right, but hear me out. Forgiveness isn't just a nicety; it is a powerful force that can bring forth healing amid despair.

Jesus showed the transformative power of forgiveness through His life and upon the cross. By forgiving those who trespassed against Him, He offered us the perfect example. Now, I'm not suggesting this is an easy path to tread. In truth, it is anything but. Pastor Thom was wounded, and his initial reaction steered him towards harbouring resentment, but let us not forget that this route merely leads to more pain. Thom decided to forgive, and he essentially broke the chains of bitterness that could bind him to Mrs Johnson. It is a decisive step towards freedom. The process of forgiving doesn't agree with the wrongdoing, nor does it deny the pain. Instead,

Pastor Thom acknowledged the hurt but choose to let go of the anger associated with it. It is a courageous act that says, 'Despite this hurt, I choose love.'

Interestingly, forgiveness has profound implications for our spiritual warfare. The enemy, Satan, thrives on division, pain, and unforgiveness. It is as if unforgiveness is the very air he breathes. When we withhold forgiveness, we inadvertently grant him space to manoeuvre, whisper lies, foster bitterness, and wreak havoc. Now, let us be practical for a moment. Forgiveness often requires a concerted effort and, in some instances, a daily recommitment.

The depth of hurt caused will often dictate the forgiveness journey's complexity. But remember, in the pursuit to heal and to disarm the schemes of Satan, forgiveness isn't an optional extra; it is an imperative.

What's more, forgiveness is deeply rooted in divine grace. The same grace that saw us through our redemption is the same grace that empowers us to forgive. As recipients of such inexplicable mercy, how can we justify withholding forgiveness? It is like a river flowing from God's throne – endless, rejuvenating, and cleansing. I've seen it repeatedly – when individuals within the church embrace forgiveness, it often sets the tone for collective healing.

For instance, when a leader forgives their accuser in the context of false accusations, it sends ripples throughout the congregation. This act can soften hearts, reconcile relationships, and restore peace. But it is essential to note that forgiveness does not equate to naivety. Being forgiving isn't tantamount to allowing repeated hurt or overlooking justice. We can – and should – still seek fairness and protection while keeping a spirit of forgiveness. It is a balance, a nuance we are called to navigate.

Forgiveness also has a mysterious way of moulding our character. Like gold refined by fire, our trials and willingness to forgive purify our hearts. This process is uncomfortable, no doubt, but the result is a heart more aligned with the heart of Christ. And isn't that the goal? One might argue, 'But the pain is too great, the wound too deep!' Indeed, the hurt can be overwhelming, and I'd never want to minimize anyone's suffering. Yet, in those darkest valleys, we can experience God's sufficiency. His grace is perfect in weakness, and His strength can move through our feeble forgiveness. Forgiveness also dismantles the barriers to communication with God.

Unforgiveness can lead to spiritual blockages – stunted growth and unanswered prayers. But when we forgive, we align ourselves with God's will, clearing the pathway for a renewed fellowship with Him. No doubt, the act of forgiveness calls for vulnerability. It is about laying down your guard, extending an olive branch even when you've been wronged. This vulnerability, however, isn't a sign of weakness. On the contrary, it proves immense spiritual strength.

And let us not forget that forgiveness is not a solitary venture. The Holy Spirit, our Counsellor and Helper, walks alongside us. He supplies the strength, patience, and courage to take each step towards complete forgiveness. With such divine companionship, who can say the task is impossible? To cap it all off, the power of forgiveness in healing isn't just about the present; it sets the tone for future relationships and circumstances. It prepares our hearts to respond with grace under fire and stand resilient in the face of future trials.

So, as we venture forward, let us not underestimate the tremendous power forgiveness holds in our collective healing and triumph over the tactics of Satan. It is a journey worth taking.

Chapter Eleven

Educating the Flock on Satan's Realities

As we turn the page from the emotional gauntlet of false accusation and the light of vindication slowly dawns, there's a crucial lesson we mustn't sidestep—it is all about recognising and understanding the guiles of the adversary, Satan. We've seen the havoc he can wreak, even within the ranks of those who mean well. It is time to consciously educate our brothers and sisters in Christ, equipping them to see beyond the veil of naivety. Think about it: if you know the ins and outs of a thief's playbook, you're less likely to fall prey to his thievery. Right?

So, we must delve into how the enemy works, expose his deceits, and shore up our defences. This isn't about fostering fear but forging a faith that's aware and alert. Armed with this knowledge, we can not only prevent the same missteps but also stand guard over one another with wisdom and discernment. So, let us press in, roll up our sleeves, and ready our hearts for some serious learning, for Satan's realities are not to be underestimated, yet they're not beyond our collective power in Christ to overcome.

Preventing Future Missteps

As we've navigated the tumultuous journey of our pastoral protagonist, we're beckoned not merely to spectate but also to actively guard against our potential pitfalls. Prevention, they say, is better than cure, and in our spiritual voyage, it is imperative to wear the whole armour of God to fend off the devil's wiles. Equipping ourselves with discernment is akin to setting up defences against a cunning adversary; it is about spotting the traps before they snap. By understanding the insidious nature of temptation and the ease with which accusations can surface, believers can stay a step ahead. It is about that internal compass, calibrated by Scripture and fellowship, which alerts us to when generosity might morph into a foothold for the enemy. This vigilant posture doesn't mean we live in paranoia but in prudent awareness, careful to shepherd our intentions and interactions with grace and wisdom, aligning our hearts with the divine blueprint for living in a fallen world often blinded to its schemes.

Equipping the Church with Knowledge

It is become abundantly clear, through Scripture and experience alike, that darkness weaves insidious threads through our lives, attempting to stain the very fabric of the church with confusion and despair. The adversary is cunning, rallying forces that run outside what the eye can perceive while curating a relentless campaign against the Christian. But it is in equipping our church with knowledge — knowledge rooted deeply in the fertile soil of Holy Scripture — that we stand vigilant and armoured against these relentless incursions.

Understanding that we are engaged in a spiritual battle is fundamental. One does not enter the fray with mere good intentions, for they alone won't stave off the well-laid snares of our spiritual opponent. The church must foster wisdom, discernment, and a robust understanding of the word of God. Scripture implores us to 'put on *the full armour of God so that you can take your stand against the devil's schemes.* This is more than a mere metaphor; it is a clarion call to take up the weapons of our warfare, which are *not carnal, but mighty through God to the pulling down of strongholds.*

Let us discuss strategy. A soldier entering battle must know the terrain, the tactics of his enemies, and the capabilities of his own arsenal. By these standards, we in the church ought to be students of spiritual terrain, familiar with the tactics Satan employs, which are documented for us in instances throughout the Bible, and wholeheartedly acquainted with the power of prayer, the strength derived from community, and the authority we wield when we stand on God's promises.

Preparing the body of believers for these unseen battles requires a touch of both shepherd and teacher. It is not enough to guide the flock with loving care; pastors must instil a scriptural literacy that surpasses the superficial within their congregations. This equipping plays out in every Bible study session, each group meeting, and the pulpit is proclamation. We must do more than just scratch the surface; we're called to dig deep and build our spiritual houses upon the bedrock of doctrinal truth.

Satan's tactics often revolve around deception, a slow and steady poisoning of truth with error. It is vital, then, to expose fables and half-truths, to teach believers not to accept every spirit but to 'test the spirits to see whether they are from God.' And how do we test them? By aligning everything against the infallible standard of Scripture to discern its veracity or deceit. Fostering a community of accountability is imperative for a church's health. A solitary believer may struggle to make out the subtle distortions of truth characteristic of the enemy's whispers. But when believers walk together, supporting one another, and giving to mutual accountability, the church functions as the unified body it is meant to be — a body far less susceptible to being divided and conquered by Satan's divisive strategies.

This readiness also involves a sober-minded approach to life's pressures and trials. Christians must recognise that while we are to expect trials, we must also understand them as opportunities to see the sanctifying hand of God at work in us, refining us like gold through fire. Trials often carry a part of spiritual combat, and our response to them either advances the cause of the Kingdom or if mishandled, provides the enemy with ammunition to use against us. Taking up the mantle of knowledge involves explicit instruction on the nature of sin and repentance. A complacent attitude towards sin undercuts our defences, making the church vulnerable. When we recognise sin for its sabotage and teach a bold, biblically sound approach to repentance and reclamation, we fortify the individual believer and the congregation at large.

We can't ignore the importance of fostering a spirit of discernment within the worship environment. Discernment isn't about fostering a sceptical community but rather about empowering each believer to perceive what's at the spiritual core of various influences, teachings, and philosophies that come their way. With such discernment, the church can navigate the relentless tide of cultural genres and ideas that often carry hidden currents opposed to the gospel. Moreover, equipping the church with knowledge includes preparing believers for the subtlety of temptation.

Pointing out that Satan rarely comes bearing plain lies but rather encroaches upon truth, subtly bending it until it breaks—this is part of a crucial defensive tactic. It often manifests in seemingly small compromises that accumulate to significant spiritual decline.

Furthermore, our knowledge should instil a profound sense of purpose and identity in Christ. When believers grasp their position as children of God and members of His royal priesthood, they're less likely to fall prey to the enemy's attempts to sow seeds of doubt about their worth and calling. This internal security is a potent deterrent against satanic schemes aimed at disillusionment and despair.

As part of our arsenal, there lies the great resource of prayer. The apostle Paul, no stranger to spiritual warfare, admonished us to pray without ceasing. Prayer is the lifeline that keeps the believer continually connected to the Commanding Officer—our God. Through prayer, we gain wisdom, power, and the peace that surpasses all understanding which guards our hearts and minds in Christ Jesus. In the end, this equipping is not intended to induce a fortress mentality, but rather to be used proactively in advancing the gospel.

We must be aware of the traps laid by the adversary but not become so inwardly focused that we neglect our mission of taking the good news to all creation. After all, 'the gates of hell shall not prevail against' a church that is both wise as serpents and innocent as doves. And let us remember, the goal is not to stir up an unhealthy preoccupation with the enemy, for our focus must ultimately rest on Christ. Instead, the purpose of 'Equipping the Church with Knowledge' is to ground us so soundly in Christ that, while we are aware of Satan's schemes, our eyes still are ever fixed on the One who has already overcome the world. In this unity of faith and knowledge, our victory in the spiritual realm is not a possibility. It is a foregone conclusion through the power of Christ within us.

So, let us press on, dear church, saturating ourselves with the word of truth, sharpening one another in love, and standing ready. For 'if God is for us, who can be against us?' With our Lord's guidance and the wisdom, He affords, we shall not merely endure but reign triumphant in the face of all adversarial tides. Equip yourselves, saints, for the battle is not just at the doorstep—it is already underfoot, and we conquer it by the Blood of the Lamb and the word of our testimony.

Chapter Twelve

Continuing the Pastoral Call

In the wake of trials that can leave a pastor's spirit bruised, the journey must go on—*Continuing the Pastoral Call* isn't just an option; it is a divine necessity. We've seen the malign shadows that can sprawl across a ministry, shadows cast not by the steeple but by the trickery of the evil one. Yet, isn't it the shepherd who, after the storm, counts his flock, binds their wounds, and leads them to green pastures once more? This chapter is about that resilience—the kind that says, although we've been battered, we can stand taller than before. It delves into anchoring oneself again in the pastoral vocation, rediscovering the joy and the challenge, the humbling and the ennobling that comes with serving the flock.

In steadfastly picking up the crook and the staff, we refuse to let our misfortunes define us or derail the work at hand. As we learn to move past our ordeals without bitterness, refocusing on ministry becomes a testament to a faith that endures, a love that forgives, and a hope that builds bridges over turbulent waters.

Moving Beyond the Ordeal
In the wake of such tumult, one's heart might feel ensnared in the thorns of tribulation, but it is in this very season that a pastor's call can't afford to waver. Moving beyond the ordeal requires resilience birthed from a deep-seated faith, indeed, the faith that acquainted us with grace in our darkest hour. As shepherds, we're beckoned to lift

our gaze from the mire of scorn and rediscover the horizon of our divine commission. This isn't a mere return to duties past; it is a transformative journey, rendering our past afflictions fertile soil for future harvests.

This pathway isn't marked by spite or a yearning for vindication; instead, it is lined with an unyielding purpose to mend the broken, to love the outcast, and to broadcast unceasingly the depth of His unending love. Let us then cast aside the weight that easily besets us and embrace, with open arms, the next chapter of unwavering ministry and relentless outreach.

Refocusing on Ministry and Outreach

As we transition towards the brighter horizon beyond our trials, it is crucial to redirect our energies towards the fundamental facets of our faith – ministry and outreach. The church, in essence, stands as a beacon of hope, a lighthouse amidst the tempestuous seas navigated by those seeking refuge and solace. This refocusing isn't merely a strategic move; it is a return to our first love, echoing the unblemished passion of the early disciples and the relentless determination they had for spreading the gospel. In the wake of our shared ordeals, there's a palpable need to re-examine what ministry means in our current context. Serving others isn't just about provision; it is about compassing the human heart with love and guiding souls to the everlasting light of Christ. As we minister, we must remember that we are not passive players in the divine narrative but active cultivators of God's kingdom on earth.

Let us not overlook the significance of outreach. It is the vigorous arm of ministry, reaching out into the darker corners of our communities where hope seems a distant dream. Our mission is to ensure that no soul is left untouched by the message of salvation. It requires creativity, resilience, and, above all, a spirit guided by

God's hand. The challenge here is keeping the delicate balance between guarding against the enemy's snares and extending open hands to those in need. Satan's schemes are often cloaked in the guise of benevolence, waiting to ensnare the unwary. But fear should not paralyse our efforts. Armed with discernment and prayer, our outreach can shield us from evil and sow seeds of faith in rocky soils.

Spiritual warfare is an unseen yet ever-present reality. As purveyors of the Good News, we step onto the battlefield with each act of kindness and word of truth. Our ministry isn't confined within the walls of our churches; it thrives in the alleyways and living rooms, wherever a heart might be crying out for redemption. Refocusing on ministry and outreach means redefining our purpose and rekindling the zealous flame that once inspired martyrs and missionaries. It is an invitation to examine closely our methods and intentions, ensuring that we point the way to Jesus in all things.

Outreach should not be haphazard but a deliberate act of planting and nurturing. Imagine each act of service as a seed, taking root in the fertile ground prepped by the Holy Spirit. We tend to these seeds, trust God's growth process, and expectantly await the harvest. The local church mustn't function as a silent monolith but as a vibrant epicentre of activity and godliness. It is through community engagement, guided by scriptural truth and prayer that we fortify our defences against Satan's ploys and lead many more to the cross, where true freedom is found.

After being targeted by the enemy, it is easy to become inward looking, focusing on our wounds and fears. But now, more than ever, the world needs the church to be outward-focused. Through refocused ministry and outreach, we heal, grow more robust, and proclaim the overwhelming conquest that is ours in Christ Jesus with renewed conviction. So, let us talk strategy. To engage effectively, we need to assess our communities' needs with spiritual lenses. This isn't just about providing for physical needs – though important – but recognising the deeper spiritual thirst that only the living water can quench.

Our actions going forward should mirror the servant heart of Jesus. He mingled among the masses, not as a distant figure, but as one who touched, spoke, and understood their plight. In embodying His example, we make the love of God absolute in a world desperate for authenticity. As we forge ahead in our ministry and outreach, it is vital to intertwine our efforts with prayer. No amount of human ingenuity can replace the power of a church on its knees, petitioning for guidance, strength, and an outpouring of the Holy Spirit.

Furthermore, there's wisdom in collaboration. Collaborating with other believers, drawing from a collective pool of gifts and insights, we become much more formidable in our quest to lead souls to salvation. Unity in purpose magnifies our abilities and fortifies our bonds in Christ. In all of this, let us not forget the value of personal witness. Each of us has a story of grace, a testament to the life-changing power of Jesus. When we share our journeys, we offer more than words – we supply a lived experience of transformation and hope.

To conclude, refocusing on ministry and outreach post-adversity isn't just a comeback; it is a battle cry. It is a declaration that while Satan might wield chaos and confusion, our God guides us with wisdom and purpose. As we move forward, let us embrace our call with humility and boldness, ever looking to the example of Christ, the perfect minister whose outreach spanned from the dusty roads of Galilee to the very ends of the earth and the depths of the human heart.

Emerging Stronger in Faith and Purpose

As we reach the end of this journey, we've marched through the darkest valleys and faced the adversary head-on, learning of his crafty manoeuvres and the subtle traps that are all too common in this tangled world. It is my hope that you now stand firmer than ever before, equipped with the sound knowledge of Satan's schemes and an emboldened faith that cannot be easily shaken. Throughout this discourse, we've seen that persecution and temptation are not just stories of old but present realities that can surface in the unlikeliest of situations.

Those kind-hearted individuals caught in the enemy's snares can appear not scathed and downtrodden but with a purpose refined by the flames of trial. It is not merely about surviving these encounters with evil but about coming out on the other side with a sharpened vision and unwavering resolve.

The trials presented serve as a stark reminder of our adversary's guile and a testament to the tenacious spirit of the Christian faith. In the heat of the battle, we often find our authentic strength in the furnace of affliction that our faith is made purer, much like gold tried in the fire. As such, we stand not as victims of circumstance but as victors over adversity.

While we've delved into instances where the faithful have suffered from injustice and false witness, we must remind ourselves that these are momentary afflictions. The pain, though piercing, is not the final stroke. In Christ, we find the strength to rise, forgive, and love, even those who stand against us. This is the remarkable nature of our calling.

When we fall prey to the darkness ever so eager to claim us, it is essential to recall the narrative of Job. Even amid profound loss and suffering, his unwavering faith serves as a beacon of hope, a reminder that divine wisdom is unfathomable and that we are to remain steadfast, patient, and trusting in God's sovereign plan. Embracing our trials, we find the courage to face false allegations with grace, navigate the complexities of legal and spiritual battles, and always hold fast to our convictions. In doing so, we must not fail to lean on our community, our Christian brothers and sisters who walk alongside us, lifting us in prayer and support.

The struggles within the body of Christ, when scandal looms near, can be deeply wounding. Yet it is here that the true power of unity and Christian love can shine brightest. As we keep our bond in Christ, addressing dissent with compassion and wisdom, we uphold the witness of the gospel and the church's integrity.

As Christian leaders, our solemn responsibility is to educate our church members on the realities of Satan's influence. Awareness is our safeguard, knowledge our shield, as we stand to prevent future missteps and strengthen those we are called to shepherd. We lead in times of peace and prosperity and amid the tempest. Continuing the pastoral call means moving beyond personal ordeals and refocusing our energies on ministry and outreach, the essence of our calling. It is about finding our stride again, not in our power but in the strength of the One we serve. Remember, our purpose is intertwined with our faith. When one is shaken, the other quivers. But strengthened anew through trials, our purpose becomes clearer, sharper — like a lighthouse cutting through the fog, guiding others towards safe shores.

So then, let us draw the curtains on our time together, not with heavy hearts but with an invigorated spirit, knowing well that the road ahead, though uncertain, is paved with divine promises. We are called to appear, not merely to endure. Our faith is the light that pierces the hollow void of deception, and our purpose is the compass that steers us ever homeward. May we take each step forward with the profound assurance that our God is mighty to save, deeply invested in our every triumph and struggle. And when the enemy's wiles appear formidable, let us hold to the unshakeable truth that greater is He in us than in the world.

So, stand firm. Let your faith be as immovable as a mountain, your purpose as relentless as the tides. We are the beacons of hope in a world often draped in shadows, the bearers of light that can never be extinguished. In Christ, and by our tenacity to hold fast to the truth, we appear stronger in faith and purpose. May you walk into tomorrow not with the dread of what might ensnare you but with the unyielding resolve to face whatever comes with dignity, strength, and an unwavering commitment to the One who has called you out of darkness into His marvellous light. To Him be glory — in our weakness, His strength is perfected, and His purposes are fulfilled in our journey.

Appendix A

Resources for the Accused

In the thick of the battle, when accusations fly like fiery darts and a reputation hangs in the balance, it is paramount that the accused know where to turn for aid. This appendix is a guiding light for those ensnared in the enemy's traps—a beacon of hope and practical help.

As Christians, prayer is the first and most powerful resource at our disposal. Reach out to the Lord, for He is close to the brokenhearted and saves those who are crushed in spirit (Psalm 34:18). Moreover, do not underestimate the strength garnered from the support of fellow believers. Involve your church elders, confide in trusted friends within the community, and let the collective prayers and wisdom envelop you like a fortress.

Simultaneously, let us not forget the vital role of legal advice in these circumstances. Seek the counsel of a reputable solicitor, one familiar with the nuances of such personal cases, so your side of the story may be articulated clearly and effectively under the law's framework. Legal aid societies or organisations specialising in religious liberties may help or point you towards those who can.

Mental well-being in these trying times is consequential, and the guidance of a professional counsellor or therapist can serve as an invaluable outlet for the emotional strain. opt for those who respect and understand the importance of your faith, for they are more likely to provide support that aligns with your values.

Additionally, it can be constructive to engage with support groups for the falsely accused. These online and in-person communities unite people who understand your plight because they've walked a mile in similar shoes. They can share strategies that worked for them and offer empathy that only those who've faced similar trials can.

Let us not neglect the treasure trove of wisdom in the pages of Christian literature that addresses false accusations and spiritual warfare. Books and articles can offer insights and perspectives that help you navigate these stormy seas. Exhaust every avenue where wisdom might be gleaned, for knowledge applied aptly is a powerful ally.

Lastly, please document everything—every interaction, correspondence, and instance related to the case. Detailed records may be your bulwark when memory falters or you need to recount accurately specific events.

Remember, although *the devil prowls around like a roaring lion looking for someone to devour* (1 Peter 5:8) you're not forsaken. Equip yourself with these resources, stay anchored in the Word, and be steadfast in hope. For in the tapestry of God's sovereign plan, even the darkest threads can highlight the brightest hues of His redeeming grace.

Appendix B

Scriptures for Comfort and Defence

So, we've journeyed together through the valleys and peaks of spiritual warfare, understanding the devious plots of the enemy and the tribulations that may come as a result. But let us not lose sight of the weaponry we've been endowed with—the comfort of scripture that both heals and defends.

When you're feeling the sting of false accusation, when whispers of deceit try to uproot your peace, remember these moments to arm yourself with the Word. Here's a compilation of scriptures that stand as pillars of strength that ward off the lies of the wicked one. It is like a shield and sword in one, right in your hands.

Comfort for the Weary Soul

Matthew 11:28-30

Come to me, all who labour and are heavy laden, and I will give you rest.

2 Corinthians 1:3-4

The Father of mercies and God of all comfort, who comforts us in all our affliction.

Psalm 23

The Lord is our Shepherd, guiding us even through the darkest valleys.

Psalm 46:1

God is our refuge and strength, a very present help in trouble.

Isaiah 41:10

Fear not, for I am with you; be not dismayed, for I am your God.

Defence Against the Enemy

Ephesians 6:10-17

A famed passage that equips us with the whole armour of God. Lean into that truth; strap on that belt of truth, the breastplate of righteousness, and take up the shield of faith.

James 4:7

'Submit yourselves therefore to God. Resist the devil, and he will flee from you.' It is a clear game plan: submit and resist.

1 Peter 5:8-9

Be sober, be vigilant; your adversary, the devil, walks about like a roaring lion, seeking whom he may devour.

A warning but also an encouragement—to stand firm in faith.

John 10:10

The thief intends to steal, kill, and destroy, our defence? Christ, who came that we may have life in abundance.

Psalm 91

A soldier's psalm affirming God's protection over us, even in the face of the enemy's arrows and schemes. And here's something to hold onto, the victory is already won. Let us not forget that Christ, with His cross, has trampled down death by death and made a spectacle of the powers of darkness. So, stand firm, friend, even when the grounds shake, and the shadows loom.

Rest assured; these scriptures aren't just mere words. They're power and life. They have weight and heft, enough to break chains and scatter lies to the winds. The next time you feel Satan's schemes nipping at your heels, declare these scriptures aloud as David did against Goliath, as Christ did in the wilderness, and watch the enemy lose his footing.

Let these scriptures sink deep into your heart, embedding them into the very fibre of your being.

Appendix C

Recognising the Spiritual Warfare Around Us

In the quiet moments that pepper our daily lives—among the whispers of doubts and the shadows of discouragement — there lurks a reality we can't ignore. It is a presence that seeks to undermine, accuse, and deceive. This is the reality of spiritual warfare. As Christians, we face an adversary adept at crafting scenarios designed to trip us up. This isn't a fairy tale; it is a genuine, ongoing battle. We must be both aware and prepared for the skirmishes and sieges we meet.

Consider the subtle moments when someone's kind words carry a twinge of malice, or a generous act is met with suspicion. Have you ever pondered that such encounters aren't just social misfortunes but might be more strategically influenced? The truth is our interactions don't take place in a vacuum. We're on a battlefield, whether we recognise it or not. Each decision and relationship exist within this greater war between good and evil.

But how can we discern what's merely a quirk of human nature from what could be a calculated move in this cosmic game? It starts by peeling back the layers, understanding that the spiritual realm influences the physical. Behind a kindly face could lurk a Judas kiss, ready to betray with a smile. It is not about becoming paranoid or distrusting everyone we meet. It is about exercising wisdom, guided by the Holy Spirit, to see beyond what's in front of us.

Remember, our opponent, Satan, isn't brandishing a pitchfork and horns. He's far more cunning. He dresses lies with the cloth of truth, and he's a master of confusion and strife. Even within the church, even among the most devout, his schemes can go unnoticed. It is why the Apostle Paul earnestly warned us to put on the whole armour of God so that we can stand against the devil's schemes. Our struggle is not against flesh and blood but against the rulers, against the authorities, against the powers of this dark world.

So, what's our strategy? Vigilance is vital, accompanied by a solid knowledge of the Word. We must be transformed by the renewal of our minds to recognise the difference between godly wisdom and human cunning. Only through close fellowship with the Lord and understanding His Word, can we start to see the subtle traps set before us, allowing us to sidestep them, remain standing, and help others do the same.

Let us be clear, though. This isn't about looking for a demon under every rock or blaming the devil for every wrong turn. We're responsible for our actions and decisions. Nevertheless, being aware of the greater spiritual context gives us insight into why things may unravel in ways we don't expect. With this knowledge, we can combat these spiritual attacks with prayer, a discerning heart, and an unwavering focus on Christ's teachings.

Understanding the reality of spiritual warfare means you won't walk into relationships and situations unarmed or naive. It means you'll discern when generosity becomes a snare, when innocence is exploited, and when sincerity is manipulated to serve ignoble ends. As daunting as this may sound, take heart. We're promised victory through Christ, who has already overcome the world. So, let us keep our eyes open, our hearts in tune with His Spirit, and march into each day with the confidence that though the battle rages on, the war is already won.

About the Author

John Amankwatia has spent his whole life serving the Lord. As a Methodist Minister, now retired, he had dedicated forty years to spreading the word of God to different communities around the United Kingdom. His passion for theology led him to earn a PhD, master's and bachelor's degrees from the universities of Birmingham, Cambridge, London. He is also the author of A Thief in My Church?